W9-BEV-638

Hip-Hop World

Hip-Hop Stars

by Sheila Griffin Llanas

Consultant:
Emmett G. Price III, PhD
Chair, Department of African American Studies
Associate Professor of Music and African American Studies
Northeastern University
Boston, Massachusetts

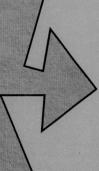

CAPSTONE PRESS
a capstone imprint

Velocity is published by Capstone Press,
151 Good Counsel Drive, P.O. Box 669, Mankato, Minnesota 56002.
www.capstonepress.com

092009
005620LKS10

 Books published by Capstone Press are manufactured with paper
containing at least 10 percent post-consumer waste.

Library of Congress Cataloging-in-Publication Data
Llanas, Sheila Griffin.
  Hip-hop stars / by Sheila Griffin Llanas.
  p. cm. — (Velocity. Hip-hop world)
  Includes bibliographical references and index.
  Summary: "Describes the birth, childhood, and career of many
hip-hop icons" — Provided by publisher.
  ISBN 978-1-4296-4019-0 (library binding)
  1. Rap musicians — United States — Biography — Juvenile literature. I. Title.
ML3929.L53 2010
782.421649092'2 — dc22   2009028165

Editorial Credits
Megan Peterson, editor; Ashlee Suker, designer; Marcie Spence, media researcher;
  Eric Manske, production specialist

Photo Credits
Alamy/DEK C, cover; Capstone Studio/Karon Dubke, 12, 15 (albums), 16 (top), 21 (top),
24, 25, 27, 33 (both), 37 (bottom), 39, 41 (right), 45 (albums); CORBIS/Mitchell Gerber,
28; Getty Images Inc./Al Pereira/Michael Oachs Archives, 16 (bottom), 17; Getty Images
Inc./David Corio/Redferns, 6, 26; Getty Images Inc./Echoes/Redferns, 8; Getty Images
Inc./Jeff Kravitz/FilmMagic, 19; Getty Images Inc./Kerstin Rodgers/Redferns, 10; Getty
Images Inc./KMazur/WireImage for New York Post, 38; Getty Images Inc./Mat Szwajkos,
20; Getty Images Inc./Michael Ochs Archives, 13; Getty Images Inc./Raymond Boyd/
Michael Ochs Archives, 23; Landov LLC/R. Marsh Starks Reuters, 41 (left); Newscom,
32, 35, 36–37 (top); Newscom/AFP Photo/Leon Neal, 45 (top); Newscom/Jeff Moreland/
CSM, 15 (bottom); Newscom/Nancy Stone/Chicago Tribune, 31; Newscom/UPI Photo/
John Angelillo, 9; Newscom/WENN, 22, 42; Rex USA/Ilpo Musto, 11; Shutterstock/
alias (old wall background throughout); Shutterstock/Anatema, 4; Shutterstock/
averole (splash element throughout); Shutterstock/Christoffer Hansen Vika, 42–43;
Shutterstock/Dusan Zidar, 7; Shutterstock/freelanceartist, 43 (top); Shutterstock/Idigital,
30; Shutterstock/kokitom (grunge background throughout); Shutterstock/Kundra (city
background throughout); Shutterstock/markhiggins, 5 (graffiti background); Shutterstock/
Neale Cousland, 21 (bottom); Shutterstock/Petrov Stanislav Eduardovich (cement wall
background throughout); Shutterstock/Pokaz (black banner throughout)

TABLE OF CONTENTS

 # Street Stars

In 1973, a Jamaican-born DJ named Kool Herc started playing music on turntables at Bronx block parties. Soon after, other DJs led the parties. They were hip-hop's first stars.

MCs, or masters of ceremonies, joined the fun. Early MCs performed at block parties. They rapped over the DJ's beats and called out rhyming lines. The audience called back. MCs got the crowd fired up.

NEW YORK CITY BOROUGHS

Bronx

Manhattan

Queens

Staten Island

Brooklyn

Breakdancers, or b-boys and b-girls, danced on their feet, hands, and backs in time to the beats. New York City crews like Rock Steady and the Dynamic Rockers competed against one another to see who had the best moves.

Graffiti artists became legends of the streets. Artists like Lady Pink and Lee Quiñones risked jail time in order to tag New York City trains, subway cars, and walls.

At first, hip-hop was about having good times at parties. Some people called it a fad. Today, hip-hop has spread beyond the boroughs of NYC. It is a way of life for people around the world. The stars in this book helped make hip-hop a global sensation.

tag	to write one's name on public property in paint or permanent marker

| borough | one of the five divisions of New York City |

Grandmaster Flash

BIRTH NAME — JOSEPH SADDLER

On New Year's Eve 1960, 2-year-old Joseph "Grandmaster Flash" Saddler snuck out of bed. He crept down the hall to spy on his parents. They were having a party. As a James Brown record played, Flash could feel each beat. He had to have more of that music.

What's in a Name?
Flash tried writing graffiti. He signed his name "Flash," after Flash Gordon cartoons. Better artists sprayed paint over his designs, but the nickname stuck.

THE ELECTRONICS OF MUSIC

Growing up in the Bronx, Grandmaster Flash loved two things — music and electronics. By the early 1970s, he was an "A" student at Samuel Gompers Vocational Technical High School in the Bronx. At home, Flash tore open his sisters' hair dryers to see how they worked. Next he took apart the washing machine, ceiling fan, stereo, and even the wall switches.

As a teenager, Flash went to neighborhood block parties. He noticed how pumped up the crowd would get when a song's instrumental break played. Flash decided to become a DJ, but he couldn't afford the equipment. Instead, he pulled stereos and speakers out of abandoned cars. Flash struck gold when he found a broken turntable in the trash. He rebuilt it and invented new ways to make a beat.

FLASH'S DEEJAYING TECHNIQUES

Grandmaster Flash invented deejaying techniques still used today:

>> **cutting** — seamlessly switching from one record to the next

>> **clock theory** — setting the needle down on the right song by marking the record with tape or crayons

GRANDMASTER FLASH AND THE FURIOUS FIVE

By the mid-1970s, Flash was deejaying all over New York City. He added five MCs to his shows to get the crowd excited. But Flash's MCs did more than shout simple phrases over the music. They wrote rhymes and even finished one another's sentences.

Eddie "Scorpio" Morris

Guy "Rahiem" Williams

Keith "Cowboy" Wiggins

Grandmaster Flash and the Furious Five

Melvin "Melle Mel" Glover

Danny "Kid Creole" Glover

Grandmaster Flash and the Furious Five became one of the first rap groups. They toured the United States and Europe. They even appeared on *Soul Train*, a popular TV show that played R&B, soul, and rap music.

RECORDING STARS

In 1979, the Sugarhill Gang released "Rapper's Delight." It was rap's first hit song. That same year, Grandmaster Flash and the Furious Five signed a recording contract with Sugar Hill Records. They released some of hip-hop's first singles:

1980 — "Freedom" is their first song to hit the radio.

1981 — "The Adventures of Grandmaster Flash on the Wheels of Steel" makes history as the first song to feature only the DJ.

1982 — "The Message" talks about inner-city life. The *New York Times* names it the most powerful single of 1982.

THE LEGACY OF GRANDMASTER FLASH

Grandmaster Flash is considered the father of modern hip-hop deejaying. He was the first DJ to play the turntables as a musical instrument. In 2007, Grandmaster Flash and the Furious Five were inducted into the Rock and Roll Hall of Fame. They were the first hip-hop group to receive this honor.

Flash's story isn't over. He continues to deejay and make music. In 2008, he wrote a book about his life called *The Adventures of Grandmaster Flash: My Life, My Beats*. He is even a character in the video game *DJ Hero*.

Rock Steady Crew

In the 1970s and 1980s, the hottest breakdancers in New York City belonged to the Rock Steady Crew. In 1977, Bronx b-boys Jimmy D and Jojo formed the Rock Steady Crew. They danced at park jams played by DJs Kool Herc, Afrika Bambaataa, and Grandmaster Flash. They competed against rivals from the five New York City boroughs. To get into the crew, b-boys and b-girls had to battle a member and win.

London Performance, 1983

Rock Steady Moves

Members of the Rock Steady Crew invented breakdancing moves that are still popular today:

>> **windmill** — a spinning move in which breakers roll their torsos on the ground while whipping their legs around in a "V" shape

>> **the 1990** — a spinning handstand using only one hand

>> **the suicide** — a flip in which the dancer lands on his or her back

WORLDWIDE FAME

In the early 1980s, the Rock Steady Crew toured England and France with DJ Afrika Bambaataa and other hip-hop artists. In 1983, they danced for the Queen of England. In 1992, the crew performed in front of President George H. W. Bush.

More than 30 years after it began, the Rock Steady Crew is still going strong. In 2007, the crew performed on the TV show *Dancing with the Stars*. Every year, the crew holds an anniversary party in the Bronx for DJs, breakdancers, graffiti artists, MCs, and hip-hop fans. As long as there's a beat, the Rocky Steady Crew will never stop busting a move.

Members of Rock Steady, 1984. Crazy Legs (far left) became president of Rock Steady in 1981.

The 1983 movie *Flashdance* starred Jennifer Beals as a woman trying to break into dancing. Rock Steady member Richard "Crazy Legs" Colon doubled as Beals for her final dance scene. He performed his famous backspin.

Run-DMC

RUN — JOSEPH SIMMONS
DMC — DARRYL McDANIELS
JAM MASTER JAY — JASON MIZELL

In 1983, two teenagers recorded songs at a friend's house in Queens, New York City. They rapped "It's Like That" and "Sucker MCs" over drums and turntables. The hard-core sound was not like anything else in hip-hop music. Would anyone like their new sound?

1984 self-titled debut album

LEGENDS IN THE MAKING

Joseph "Run" Simmons and Darryl "DMC" McDaniels went to school together in Queens. They shared a love for rap music. Run deejayed at his big brother Russell's parties. DMC played the turntables. They both wrote rhymes. In the early 1980s, the two friends formed the rap group Run-DMC.

Run's brother sold Run-DMC's singles "It's Like That" and "Sucker MCs" to Profile Records in 1983. Soon, Run-DMC's songs were getting daytime radio play. Back then, rap music usually was played at night when people were asleep. "It's Like That" sold a total of 250,000 copies. Run-DMC's new sound caught on fast. They soon added Jason "Jam Master Jay" Mizell to the group. Jam Master Jay was a DJ who also played the guitar and drums.

NEW SCHOOL RAP

Until the mid-1980s, "old school" rap music used funk and disco styles. The upbeat sound was often played for parties. Run-DMC rapped over drum machines and a turntable to create a new, hard-hitting sound. The new sound was called "new school."

words with a message + sparse beats + a heavy metal twist = new school

Jam Master Jay

DMC

Run

In 1985, Run-DMC starred in the hip-hop movie *Krush Groove*. Kurtis Blow, the Beastie Boys, and the Fat Boys also appeared in the film.

RAP BREAKS INTO MAINSTREAM MUSIC

Run-DMC liked to rap over rock records, including "Walk This Way" by the band Aerosmith. Then Run-DMC got the idea to rap Aerosmith's song. In 1986, the two bands recorded "Walk This Way" together. Aerosmith and Run-DMC crashed through a wall to reach each other in the music video. Rock and hip-hop fans got the message — it was okay to like both styles of music. "Walk This Way" was the first rap single to reach *Billboard's* top-10 pop chart.

RUN-DMC'S FIRSTS

» *Raising Hell* was rap's first platinum album.

» In 1987, *Raising Hell* was the first rap album to earn a Grammy nomination.

» Run-DMC was the first rap group to appear on the cover of the popular *Rolling Stone* magazine.

» Run-DMC's video for "Rock Box" was the first rap video played on MTV.

A Grammy is an award presented by The Recording Academy to top recording artists. Each year, academy members vote for their favorites in styles such as rap, rock, pop, and country.

RUN-DMC ALBUMS

Run-DMC (1984)

King of Rock (1985)

Raising Hell (1986)

Tougher Than Leather (1988)

Back from Hell (1990)

Down with the King (1993)

Crown Royal (2001)

ALBUM RANKS

An album's rank is based on the number of U.S. sales. The Recording Industry Association of America tracks sales and makes the awards.

Albums Sold	Rank
500,000	Gold
1 million	Platinum
10 million	Diamond

Only three hip-hop albums have been certified diamond.

» MC Hammer - *Please Hammer Don't Hurt 'Em*, 1990

» The Notorious B.I.G. - *Life After Death*, 1997

» OutKast - *Speakerboxxx/The Love Below*, 2003

In 2009, Run-DMC was inducted into the Rock and Roll Hall of Fame. They are only the second hip-hop group to receive this honor. "They were the first rock stars of rap," Eminem said at the induction ceremony. "None of us would be here without them."

Salt-N-Pepa

SALT — CHERYL JAMES
PEPA — SANDY DENTON
DJ SPINDERELLA — DEE DEE ROPER

Cheryl "Salt" James and Sandy "Pepa" Denton never set out to be rappers. In 1985, they were nursing students at Queensborough Community College. To make money, they worked together at Sears. When a coworker invited them to rap on a song he wrote, they stepped up to the microphone. Their career plans were about to change.

Salt

Pepa

sample ❯❯ *to take a portion of one song and reuse it in another*

DJ Spinderella

Salt-N-Pepa released their first single, "The Show Stopper," under the name Super Nature.

STARTING OUT

Pepa and Salt met in their college cafeteria. Pepa, playful and outgoing, noticed Salt reading by herself in the corner. They soon became friends and started working together at Sears. Around that time, "The Show" by Doug E. Fresh and Slick Rick was a popular rap song. Salt and Pepa's coworker, Hurby Azor, wrote a response song called "The Show Stopper." In the song, Salt and Pepa poked fun at Doug E. Fresh and Slick Rick.

"The Show Stopper" became popular on the radio. Salt and Pepa quickly got into the studio to record more songs. **Sampling** from upbeat music like Otis Redding and the Kinks, they recorded the singles "Tramp" and "Push It." They also added Dee Dee "DJ Spinderella" Roper to the group. Their first album, *Hot Cool & Vicious*, debuted in 1986. It sold 1 million copies.

Salt-N-Pepa's Success

>> "Push It" earned one of rap's first Grammy nominations for Best Rap Performance by a Duo or Group in 1989.

>> The 1993 album *Very Necessary* sold 5 million copies. It remains the best-selling album by a female rap group.

>> The hit song "None of Your Business" won a Grammy Award for Best Rap Performance in 1994.

Hip-Hop's First "Diss" Song

In 1985, rap group U.T.F.O. released "Roxanne, Roxanne." The song is about a girl who wouldn't give a guy any attention. Roxanne Shante, a 15-year-old from Queens, responded with the song "Roxanne's Revenge." That was the first "diss" or disrespect record. The song inspired a hip-hop tradition of song battling.

Salt-N-Pepa Albums

Hot Cool & Vicious (1986)

A Salt with a Deadly Pepa (1988)

Black's Magic (1990)

Very Necessary (1993)

Brand New (1997)

Life after rap

Salt-N-Pepa released their final album, *Brand New*, in 1997. After a string of hits, they wanted to try new things. Salt recorded a solo album, *Salt Unrapped*. Pepa wrote a book about her life called *Let's Talk About Pep*. Spinderella hosts a radio show called *The Backspin*. In 2007, Salt-N-Pepa produced a reality TV show for VH1 called *The Salt-N-Pepa Show*. Whatever they do, Salt-N-Pepa remains one of hip-hop's greatest groups.

Lady Pink

BIRTH NAME — SANDRA FABARA

Sandra "Lady Pink" Fabara started writing graffiti in 1979 at age 15. She was one of the only female graffiti writers. Lady Pink had to prove she was tough enough to hang with the boys. That meant hauling heavy bags of spray paint into the dark and dangerous train yards of New York City.

Lady Pink developed her art talent early in life. She attended the High School of Art and Design in Manhattan. At school, Lady Pink met other graffiti writers. She practiced her graffiti skills in the bathroom of her school. She soon began painting subway cars, an illegal activity.

LADY PINK'S STYLE

Every graffiti writer has his or her own style. Lady Pink uses light colors, such as pink and purple. She designs women, flowers, and landscapes.

THE ART SCENE

Lady Pink was just 21 years old when she had her first solo art show at the Moore College of Art. Since then her work has been shown in museums around the world. She was one of the only female graffiti artists featured in the 1984 book *Subway Art*. Today, Lady Pink owns a mural company in New York City. She continues to paint and teach graffiti art.

Lady Pink played a graffiti writer in the 1982 classic hip-hop film *Wild Style*.

Tupac Shakur

Tupac Shakur was raised by a family of activists. His mother, Afeni, was a member of the Black Panthers. This group fought for better treatment of African-Americans. As a kid, Tupac and his family moved between the Bronx and Harlem.

Intelligent and quiet, Tupac enjoyed the arts. He read, kept a diary, and enjoyed acting. At age 12, he joined a Harlem theater group. He played the role of Travis in *A Raisin in the Sun* at the Apollo Theatre.

In 1986, Tupac moved to Baltimore, Maryland, with his mother and younger sister. Tupac studied acting, dance, and art at the Baltimore School for the Arts. While in school, Tupac decided he wanted to be a rap artist. He started writing rap lyrics at age 15. In 1988, his family moved across the country to Marin City, California. His mother wanted a new start, but Tupac missed his old school and friends.

Tupac with this mother, Afeni

activist	a person who supports a cause such as equality

TuPac BREAKS iNto MuSic

In the early 1990s, Tupac joined a rap group called Digital Underground. They hired him to help set up their concerts. They also let him record rap vocals on a few of their songs. Meanwhile, Tupac made a demo tape of his own. It reached a producer at Interscope Records. They were impressed and offered Tupac a recording contract.

Tupac wanted his album to make a difference. In his deep voice, Tupac belted out his views on politics and society. He rapped about the violence, poverty, teen pregnancy, and illegal drug use he saw growing up. He released his first album, *2Pacalypse Now*, in 1991. The album eventually went gold.

While living in Baltimore, Tupac called himself MC New York. He thought the name made him sound tough.

CAREER SUCCESS

Tupac's music and acting career took off soon after his first album hit store shelves. He starred in successful films and released his second album in 1993. In November 1994, Tupac went to visit his friend, the Notorious B.I.G., at a studio in New York City. But Tupac never made it past the lobby. He was shot and robbed.

Tupac recovered from his injuries and focused on his music. In 1995, he released the album *Me Against the World*. It earned a Grammy nomination for Best Rap Album.

TUPAC'S FILM ROLES

From rapping to acting to writing poetry, Tupac enjoyed expressing himself in artistic ways. Here are just a few of Tupac's film roles:

>> *Juice*, 1992. Tupac played the character of Bishop, a violent teen living in New York City.

>> *Poetic Justice*, 1993. Acting alongside Janet Jackson, Tupac played Lucky, a mailman who falls for Jackson's character.

>> *Above the Rim*, 1994. Tupac starred as Birdie, a club owner. Birdie convinces a high school basketball whiz to play for his street team.

TUPAC SHAKUR ALBUMS

2Pacalypse Now (1991)

Strictly 4 My N***** (1993)

Thug Life, Vol I (1994)

Me Against the World (1995)

All Eyez on Me (1996)

The Don Killuminati: The 7 Day Theory (1996)

R U Still Down? (Remember Me) (1997)

Until the End of Time (2001)

2PAC

all eyez on me

All Eyez on Me made history as hip-hop's first double-disc album of original material.

TUPAC'S DEATH

On September 7, 1996, Tupac went to a boxing match in Las Vegas, Nevada. While driving back to his hotel, he was shot several times. He died on September 13 at age 25. His murder was never solved. Tupac remains the top-selling rap artist in the United States.

The Notorious B.I.G.

BiRtH NAME — CHRiStoPHER GEORGE LEtORE WALLACE

In 1992, Christopher "the Notorious B.I.G." Wallace recorded a demo tape. He rapped for fun but didn't expect to get a record deal out of it. Then his friend sent the tape to *The Source*, a hip-hop magazine. They printed a great review of his tape. Music producer Sean "Diddy" Combs read the review and listened to the tape. The Notorious B.I.G. was about to hit the big time.

GROWING UP IN BROOKLYN

As an only child, the Notorious B.I.G., also called Biggie Smalls, was close to his mother. At more than 6 feet (1.8 meters) tall and weighing 300 pounds (136 kilograms), he was shy, funny, and smart. In elementary school, Biggie won awards for his reading, math, and English skills. He often played video games with his friends at his house.

Biggie enjoyed music from a young age. His mother was from Jamaica, and they traveled there each summer. Biggie liked the reggae music he heard while on the island.

In Brooklyn, Biggie rapped with different hip-hop groups. He also competed against other rappers in his neighborhood. Biggie almost always won. Diddy signed Biggie to a recording contract with Bad Boy Records after hearing his demo tape in 1992.

Diddy worked with Biggie to find his rap style. Biggie's songs told personal stories. They spilled the truth about street life. But Diddy convinced Biggie to tone down the violence. Biggie rapped in a smooth, confident style. In 1994, Biggie released his first album, *Ready to Die*.

A B.I.G. DEBut

Biggie's debut album, *Ready to Die*, got a lot of buzz.

» "Big Poppa" earned a Grammy nomination for Best Rap Solo Performance.

» *Ready to Die* sold 4 million albums.

» In 2006, *Time* magazine listed *Ready to Die* as one of the 100 greatest albums of all time.

the notorious BIG

ready to die

BiggiE'S M.A.F.I.A.

Biggie promised his childhood friends he would help them make a record once he became successful. Biggie kept his word. In 1995, he and his friends formed the Junior M.A.F.I.A. — Masters At Finding Intelligent Attitudes. They released the album *Conspiracy*. Biggie then helped Lil' Kim, the group's only female, make her solo album *Hardcore*.

Lil' Kim

Biggie

Diddy

THE NOTORIOUS B.I.G. ALBUMS

Ready to Die (1994)

Life After Death (1997)

Born Again (1999)

Duets: The Final Chapter (2005)

Greatest Hits (2007)

Biggie rarely wrote down his rhymes. In the recording studio, he rhymed the lyrics from memory.

MTV's Greatest MCs of All Time

MTV's 2006 list of the Greatest MCs of All Time sparked a heated debate among hip-hop fans. Even the MCs themselves weighed in. Each had a different list, proving that MC ranking is a personal thing.

MTV's Top-10 Greatest MCs of All Time:

- » 1. Jay-Z
- » 2. Tupac Shakur
- » 3. The Notorious B.I.G.
- » 4. Rakim
- » 5. Nas
- » 6. KRS-One
- » 7. Big Daddy Kane
- » 8. Ice Cube
- » 9. Eminem
- » 10. LL Cool J

Life After Death

In 1997, Biggie got back into the studio to record his second album, *Life After Death*. With 24 songs, it was a double-disc album. He visited Los Angeles to promote the album. While in L.A., he and Diddy attended a party. Biggie was shot to death while driving back to his hotel. He died on March 9, 1997, at age 24. His murder remains unsolved.

Life After Death was released two weeks after Biggie's death. The album became one of the three hip-hop albums certified as diamond. It also earned a Grammy nomination for Best Rap Album.

In his short career, the Notorious B.I.G. helped make Bad Boy Records a success. He also passed his good fortune onto his childhood friends. He remains one of the most popular rap artists ever to cut a record.

Eminem

Marshall "Eminem" Mathers III entered a recording studio in 1996 to cut his debut album, *Infinite*. A small Detroit record label released the album. But it didn't sell. Critics said Eminem tried to sound like African-American rap artists. It seemed as though his dream of becoming a rap star was fading fast.

CHILDHOOD IN DETROIT

Eminem grew up in the suburbs of Detroit, Michigan. The eldest of two sons, Eminem wanted to be a comic book artist and a rapper. He listened to rappers like Dr. Dre and Ice Cube. In high school, Eminem rapped in MC contests at the Hip-Hop Shop in Detroit. He also formed a hip-hop crew with some of his friends called D12.

What's in a Name?
Eminem originally spelled his nickname M&M. He later spelled out those initials to create Eminem.

EminEm InVEnts Slim Shady

Eminem was disappointed by the failure of *Infinite*. In the summer of 1997, he invented the character of Slim Shady. He vented his emotions through the voice of this character. Eminem found a notebook and started writing new songs, which he recorded on a demo tape.

Dr. Dre

Eminem

EminEm's Big BREAK

In 1997, Eminem saved up enough money to go the Rap Olympics in Los Angeles. Each year, MCs competed against one another at this freestyle rap contest. Eminem wanted to prove he had the skills to be a successful rapper. He came in second.

Soon after the Rap Olympics, Eminem's demo tape reached Dr. Dre at Interscope Records. Dr. Dre listened to the tape and said, "Find him. Now." Eminem recorded *The Slim Shady LP*, which hit the shelves in 1999. It sold 4 million copies and stayed on *Billboard's* Top 200 albums chart for almost two years. He followed up with *The Marshall Mathers LP* in 2000. This album was an even bigger success, selling close to 2 million copies in its first week of release.

EMINEM'S RAP STYLE

>> Eminem uses a mix of humor and anger in his lyrics.

>> He also mixes fantasy superheroes with real-life stories.

>> Eminem uses "insider" rhymes. This style includes rhyming words within each line as well as at the ends of lines.

Eminem's video for "The Real Slim Shady" won the MTV Video Music Award for Best Male Video and Video of the Year in 2000.

The Slim Shady LP, The Marshall Mathers LP, and The Eminem Show each won the Grammy for Best Rap Album.

EMINEM ALBUMS

Infinite (1996)

The Slim Shady LP (1999)

The Marshall Mathers LP (2000)

The Eminem Show (2002)

Encore (2004)

Relapse (2009)

FROM RAP to tHE BiG SCREEN

In 2002, Eminem starred in the movie *8 Mile*. The film was loosely based on his life. During a break from filming, Eminem scribbled the lyrics to "Lose Yourself," the film's theme song. The song won an Academy Award for Best Original Song. Eminem became the first rapper to win an Academy Award for songwriting.

In 2008, *Vibe* magazine readers voted Eminem the Best Rapper Alive. He beat out Jay-Z to win the title.

Missy Elliott

BIRTH NAME — MELISSA ARNETTE ELLIOTT

While still a teenager, Missy Elliott decided to pursue a singing career. But she didn't join a group — she formed one. Missy created an R&B group called Sista. She wrote all of their songs. From the start, Missy always took full control of her own music.

GROWING UP MISSY

Missy grew up an only child in Jacksonville, North Carolina, and Portsmouth, Virginia. From a young age, she enjoyed singing. Missy belted out Jackson 5 songs and performed "concerts," using her dolls as an "audience." She sang in a church choir and wrote song lyrics on her bedroom walls. At school, Missy rarely completed her assignments. But when the school gave her an IQ test, Missy passed as a genius.

Missy's home life was sometimes difficult. At age 14, she and her mother left her abusive father. Missy found her hip-hop role models in Salt-N-Pepa. That's when Missy knew she wanted to be a rapper.

SuPa DuPa DEBut

Missy's neighborhood friend Timothy "Timbaland" Mosley produced songs for Missy's band Sista. Sista released one single called "Brand New" in 1994. But their deal with Swing Mob Records soon fell through.

Missy then focused on writing music. Missy and Timbaland wrote and produced most of the songs on Aaliyah's 1996 album *One in a Million*. After the success of Aaliyah's album, Missy was flooded with recording offers. But she wanted control over her own career. She created the record label Gold Mind, Inc. With Timbaland producing, Missy recorded her debut album. She rapped steadily over R&B and futuristic beats. *Supa Dupa Fly* hit stores in 1997. It went on to sell more than 1 million copies and earned a Grammy nomination for Best Rap Album.

Missy Elliott is the only solo female rapper to have six records certified platinum.

MiSSY'S StYLE

Missy has her own unique fashion style. She loves sneakers and even wore them to her first Grammy ceremony. In 2004, Missy teamed up with Adidas to create her own clothing line for women called Respect M.E. It features sneakers, T-shirts, jackets, and tracksuits.

In her video for "The Rain," Missy wore an inflated garbage bag. That costume is now in the Rock and Roll Hall of Fame.

MiSSY'S GRAMMY WiNS

Missy's talents as a rapper and producer have earned her more than 20 Grammy nominations. Check out her Grammy wins:

>> **2001** — Best Rap Solo Performance for "Get Ur Freak On"

>> **2002** — Best Female Rap Solo Performance for "Scream a.k.a. Itchin'"

>> **2003** — Best Female Rap Solo Performance for "Work It"

>> **2005** — Best Short Form Music Video for "Lose Control"

MISSY ELLIOTT ALBUMS

Supa Dupa Fly (1997)

Da Real World (1999)

Miss E ... So Addictive (2001)

Under Construction (2002)

This is Not a Test (2003)

The Cookbook (2005)

Missy found success as a top-selling rap star, but she never forgot her past. In 2003, she became a spokesperson for Break the Cycle. This organization fights domestic violence.

Jay-Z

Shawn "Jay-Z" Carter's 2003 farewell concert sold out in one day. The star-studded event took place in Madison Square Garden, an arena not far from where Jay-Z grew up. Missy Elliott, Mary J. Blige, and Beyoncé performed. All proceeds from the concert went to charity. A film was made of that legendary concert called *Fade to Black*. If this were the end of his rap career, Jay-Z wanted to go out in high style.

Mary J. Blige

What's in a Name?
Jay-Z is short for Jazzy, his childhood nickname.

38

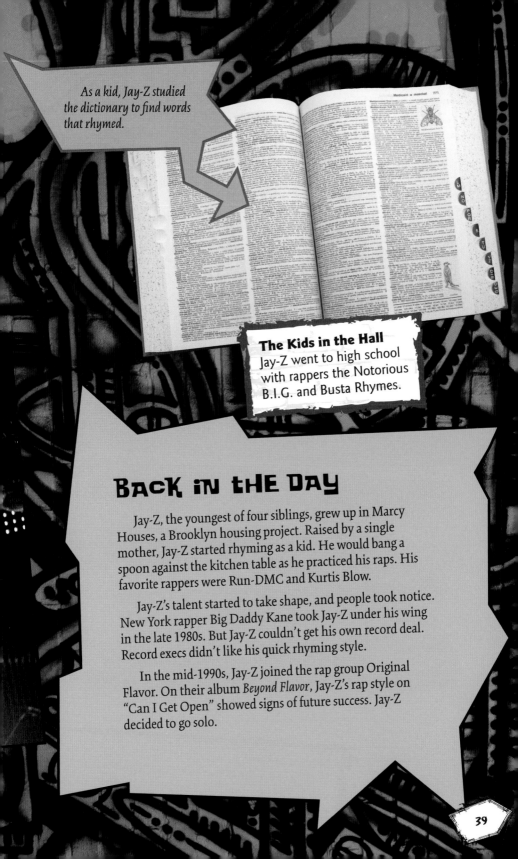

As a kid, Jay-Z studied the dictionary to find words that rhymed.

The Kids in the Hall
Jay-Z went to high school with rappers the Notorious B.I.G. and Busta Rhymes.

BACK IN THE DAY

Jay-Z, the youngest of four siblings, grew up in Marcy Houses, a Brooklyn housing project. Raised by a single mother, Jay-Z started rhyming as a kid. He would bang a spoon against the kitchen table as he practiced his raps. His favorite rappers were Run-DMC and Kurtis Blow.

Jay-Z's talent started to take shape, and people took notice. New York rapper Big Daddy Kane took Jay-Z under his wing in the late 1980s. But Jay-Z couldn't get his own record deal. Record execs didn't like his quick rhyming style.

In the mid-1990s, Jay-Z joined the rap group Original Flavor. On their album *Beyond Flavor*, Jay-Z's rap style on "Can I Get Open" showed signs of future success. Jay-Z decided to go solo.

Roc-A-Fella

When deals with record companies continued to fall through, Jay-Z made a bold move for a new artist. He formed his own company, Roc-A-Fella Records. Jay-Z released his debut album, *Reasonable Doubt*, in 1996. He rapped about his life in the projects. Mary J. Blige, the Notorious B.I.G., and Foxy Brown guest rapped on the album. But his breakout album was yet to come.

Jay-Z was at a club when he got an idea for a new song. He heard a DJ spin "It's the Hard-Knock Life" from the musical *Annie*. Jay-Z felt the song spoke to his own experiences growing up in the projects. He made the song his own and released his third album, *Vol. 2. . .Hard Knock Life*, in 1998. "Hard Knock Life (Ghetto Anthem)" helped make the album a hit with fans. It sold more than 5 million copies and won the Grammy for Best Rap Album.

Jay-Z the Businessman

Jay-Z is considered one of the greatest rappers of all time. He is also a successful businessman. Check out some of his business ventures:

» Owner of the 40/40 Club located in New York City, Atlantic City, Las Vegas, Chicago, Japan, and China

» Creator of Rocawear, one of hip-hop's top fashion lines

» Part owner of the New Jersey Nets basketball team

» First non-athlete to have a line of Reebok sneakers called the S. Carter Collection

School is Cool
Jay-Z created the Shawn Carter Scholarship Fund in 2003. This fund provides college scholarships for high school graduates in the Marcy Projects area.

JAY-Z ALBUMS

Reasonable Doubt (1996)

In My Lifetime, Vol. I (1997)

Vol. 2 ... Hard Knock Life (1998)

Vol. 3 ... Life and Times of S. Carter (1999)

The Dynasty: Roc La Familia (2000)

The Blueprint (2001)

The Blueprint²: The Gift & the Curse (2002)

The Black Album (2003)

Kingdom Come (2006)

American Gangster (2007)

The Blueprint³ (2009)

OUT OF RETIREMENT

After his 2003 farewell concert, Jay-Z decided not to retire. He felt he still had more to offer the world of hip-hop music. Jay-Z continued to put out chart-topping rap albums. In 2008, he teamed up with rappers T.I., Kanye West, and Lil Wayne to record the single "Swagga Like Us." The song won a Grammy Award for Best Rap Performance by a Duo or Group.

Jay-Z began as an underground rapper with no record deal. He turned himself into a hip-hop **mogul**. No wonder MTV voted Jay-Z the Greatest MC of All Time.

mogul ⟩⟩ *an important or powerful person*

Kanye West

Kanye West met with Roc-A-Fella Records producers in 2002. He stood before them dressed in a pink polo shirt and Gucci loafers. Kanye wanted to make a rap album. He didn't look like a typical rap artist, but he had talent. He worked for Roc-A-Fella and produced hits for superstar Jay-Z. Still, record executives weren't sure he could make it as a rap artist.

Kanye and his mother, Donda West

Kanye loves fashion. He made the *Vanity Fair* International Best-Dressed List in 2006 and 2008.

In 2007, Kanye owned the world's first pair of Shutter Shades. Since then, the shades have become popular hip-hop fashion.

THE WINDY CITY

Kanye West was born in Atlanta, Georgia, and grew up in Chicago, Illinois. He is the only child of divorced parents. Growing up, Kanye traveled a lot. He lived with his mother, a college professor. He spent his summers with his dad, a former Black Panther, photographer, and church counselor. He even lived in China for a year with his mom while she taught English.

Kanye started rapping and making his own beats in elementary school. He wanted to pursue a music career, but his parents wanted him to go to college. Kanye finished one year of art school at Chicago State University. With dreams of making it in music, Kanye then moved to New York City. In 2001, he got a job at Roc-A-Fella Records.

Roc-A-Fella Dreams

Kanye found success at Roc-A-Fella Records. He composed five songs for Jay-Z's 2001 album *The Blueprint*. Kanye also produced singles for stars like Alicia Keys and Ludacris. Still, Kanye had dreams of making an album of his own.

Kanye's life changed forever in October 2002. He was driving home one night when he had a car accident. His jaw broke in three places. While recovering from his accident, Kanye wrote and recorded a song called "Through the Wire." He rapped the vocals with his jaw wired shut. Kanye proved to Roc-A-Fella that he had the talent to make it as a rapper. His 2004 debut album, *The College Dropout*, earned an amazing 10 Grammy nominations. It also won the Grammy for Best Rap Album.

Kanye's Musical Style

>> The Samples — Kanye samples from songs by artists such as the Jackson 5, Elton John, the Temptations.

>> The Process — He speeds up the track and lays drums and rap vocals over a high-pitched sound.

GOOD Music
Kanye started his own record label called GOOD Music (Getting Out Our Dreams). He has signed artists such as John Legend and Common.

KANYE WEST ALBUMS

The College Dropout (2004)

Late Registration (2005)

Graduation (2007)

808s & Heartbreak (2008)

Graduation

In 2005, *Time* magazine listed Kanye as one of the 100 most influential people in the world. He has been credited with bringing social awareness back into hip-hop lyrics. Kanye is a performer, producer, writer, and record executive. His full legacy is yet to be known, but Kanye West is already a hip-hop superstar.

GLOSSARY

activist (AK-ti-vist) — a person who supports a cause such as equality

borough (BUHR-oh) — one of the five divisions of New York City, each of which is also a county

breakdance (BRAYK-danss) — a form of street dance that features footwork, floor work, and other acrobatic moves

debut (DAY-byoo) — to present to the public for the first time

deejay (DEE-jay) — to play pre-recorded music for a radio, party, or club audience

graffiti (gruh-FEE-tee) — letters or pictures painted, scratched, or marked onto a piece of public property

MC (em-SEE) — a person who rhymes to the DJ's mix, connecting with the audience in a performance

mogul (MOW-guhl) — an important or powerful person

pitch (PICH) — the highness of lowness of a sound

sample (SAM-puhl) — to take a portion of one song and reuse it in another

tag (TAYG) — to write one's name on public property in paint or permanent marker

turntable (TURN-tay-buhl) — a circular, revolving surface used for playing phonograph records

READ MORE

Collins, Tracy Brown. *Missy Elliott.* Hip-Hop Stars. New York: Chelsea House, 2007.

Garofoli, Wendy. *Hip-Hop History.* Hip-Hop World. Mankato, Minn.: Capstone Press, 2010.

Slavicek, Louise Chipley. *Run-DMC.* Hip-Hop Stars. New York: Chelsea House, 2007.

Weicker, Gretchen. *Kanye West: Hip-Hop Star.* Hot Celebrity Biographies. Berkeley Heights, N.J.: Enslow, 2009.

INTERNET SITES

FactHound offers a safe, fun way to find Internet sites related to this book. All of the sites on FactHound have been researched by our staff.

Here's all you do:

Visit *www.facthound.com*

FactHound will fetch the best sites for you!

INDEX